First hundred words in Portuguese

Heather Amery

Illustrated by Stephen Cartwright

Translation and pronunciation guide by
Octávio Gameiro and Richard Correll

Designed by Mike Olley and Jan McCafferty

D0177351

 There is a little yellow duck to find in every picture.

A sala de estar The living room

o papá
Daddy

a mamã
Mummy

o menino
boy

2

a menina
girl

o bebé
baby

o cão
dog

o gato
cat

3

A roupa Clothes

os sapatos
shoes

as cuecas
pants

o pulôver
jumper

4

a camisola
interior
vest

as calças
trousers

a T-shirt
t-shirt

as meias
socks

A cozinha   The kitchen

o pão
bread

o leite
milk

os ovos
eggs

6

a maçã
apple

a laranja
orange

a banana
banana

A lavagem de louça — Washing up

a mesa
table

a cadeira
chair

o prato
plate

a faca
knife

o garfo
fork

a colher
spoon

a chávena
cup

Os brinquedos Toys

o cavalo
horse

a ovelha
sheep

a vaca
cow

a galinha
hen

o porco
pig

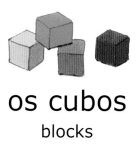

o comboio
train

os cubos
blocks

Uma visita   A visit

a avó
Granny

o avô
Grandpa

as pantufas
slippers

12

o casaco
coat

o vestido
dress

o chapéu
hat

O parque The park

a árvore
tree

a flor
flower

os baloiços
swings

a bola
ball

14

o escorrega
slide

as botas
boots

o pássaro
bird

o barco
boat

A rua The street

o carro
car

a bicicleta
bicycle

o avião
plane

o camião
truck

o autocarro
bus

a casa
house

17

A festa The party

o balão
balloon

o bolo
cake

o relógio
clock

o gelado
ice cream

o peixe
fish

as bolachas
biscuits

os rebuçados
sweets

19

A piscina   The swimming pool

o braço
arm

a mão
hand

a perna
leg

os pés
feet

os dedos dos pés
toes

a cabeça
head

o rabinho
bottom

21

O vestiário   The changing room

a boca
mouth

os olhos
eyes

as orelhas
ears

o nariz
nose

o cabelo
hair

o pente
comb

a escova
brush

A loja   The shop

vermelho
red

azul
blue

verde
green

24

amarelo
yellow

cor-de-rosa
pink

branco
white

preto
black

A casa de banho The bathroom

o sabonete
soap

a toalha
towel

a sanita
toilet

2

o banho
bath

a barriga
tummy

o patinho
duck

O quarto The bedroom

a cama
bed

o candeeiro
lamp

a janela
window

28

a porta
door

o livro
book

a boneca
doll

o urso de peluche
teddy

Match the words to the pictures

a banana

a bola

o bolo

a boneca

as botas

a camisola
   interior

o candeeiro

o cão

o carro

o chapéu

o comboio

a faca

o garfo

o gato

o gelado

a janela

a laranja

o leite

o livro

a maçã

as meias

a mesa

o ovo

o patinho

o peixe

o porco

o pulôver

o relógio

o urso de peluche

a vaca

31

Os números Numbers

1 um/uma
one

2 dois
two

3 três
three

4 quatro
four

5 cinco
five

1 um/uma
one

2 dois
two

3 três
three

4 quatro
four

5 cinco
five

Word list

In this alphabetical list of all the words in the pictures, the Portuguese word comes first, next is a guide to saying the word, and then there is the English translation. The guide may look strange or funny, but just try to read the words as if they were English.

Most Portuguese words have a part that you stress, or say louder (like the "day" part of the English word "today"). So you know which part of each word you should stress, it is shown in letters **like this** in the pronunciation guide.

It will help you to say the words in Portuguese correctly if you remember these things about the way Portuguese is said:

- when you see *(n)* in the pronunciation guide, you should barely say it; say the letter that is before it through your nose, as if you have a cold

- *ow* is always pronounced as in d*ow*n

- the Portuguese *r* is pronounced more strongly than in English, especially at the end of a word; try rolling it a little, *rrr*

- when you see *zh*, say it like the *s* in treasure

amarelo	*ama**re**loo*	yellow
a árvore	*eh **ar**voreh*	tree
o autocarro	*oo owtoo**carr**oo*	bus
o avião	*oo avee**ow(n)***	plane
a avó	*eh a**voh***	Granny
o avô	*oo a**voo***	Grandpa
azul	*a**zool***	blue
o balão	*oo ba**low(n)***	balloon
os baloiços	*oozh ba**loy**sush*	swings
a banana	*eh ba**na**na*	banana
o banho	*oo **ban**yoo*	bath
o barco	*oo **bar**coo*	boat
a barriga	*eh bar**ree**ga*	tummy
o bebé	*oo be**bay***	baby
a bicicleta	*eh beesee**cle**ta*	bicycle
a boca	*eh **bo**ca*	mouth
a bola	*eh **boh**la*	ball
as bolachas	*ezh bo**la**shash*	biscuits
o bolo	*oo **boh**loo*	cake
a boneca	*eh bo**ne**ca*	doll
as botas	*ezh **boh**tash*	boots
o braço	*oo **bra**soo*	arm
branco	***bran**coo*	white
os brinquedos	*oozh brin**kay**doosh*	toys
a cabeça	*eh ca**bes**sa*	head
o cabelo	*oo ca**beh**loo*	hair
a cadeira	*eh ca**day**ra*	chair

as calças	*esh **cal**sesh*	trousers
a cama	*eh **ca**ma*	bed
o camião	*oo cami**ow(n)***	truck
a camisola interior	*eh camee**zoh**la eenter**yor***	vest
o candeeiro	*oo candy-**ay**roo*	lamp
o cão	*oo **cow(n)***	dog
o carro	*oo **carr**oo*	car
a casa	*eh **ca**za*	house
a casa de banho	*eh **ca**za de **ban**yoo*	bathroom
o casaco	*oo ca**za**koo*	coat
o cavalo	*oo ca**va**loo*	horse
o chapéu	*oo sha**pay**oo*	hat
a chávena	*eh **shah**vena*	cup
cinco	***sin**coo*	five
a colher	*eh co**lyair***	spoon
o comboio	*oo com**boy**oo*	train
cor-de-rosa	*cor-de-**roh**za*	pink
a cozinha	*eh cu**zee**nya*	kitchen
os cubos	*oosh **coo**boosh*	blocks
as cuecas	*esh **kwek**ash*	pants
os dedos dos pés	*oozh **de**doosh doosh **pehsh***	toes
dois	***doysh***	two
o escorrega	*oo eshkor**ray**ga*	slide
a escova	*eh esh**ko**va*	brush

33

Portuguese	Pronunciation	English
a faca	eh **fa**ca	knife
a festa	eh **fesh**ta	party
a flor	eh **flor**	flower
a galinha	eh ga**lee**nya	hen
o garfo	oo **gar**foo	fork
o gato	oo **ga**too	cat
o gelado	oo zhe**lah**doo	ice cream
a janela	eh zha**ne**la	window
a laranja	eh la**ran**zha	orange
a lavagem de louça	eh la**va**zhem de **loy**sa	washing up
o leite	oo **layt**	milk
o livro	oo **lee**vroo	book
a loja	eh **lo**zha	shop
a maçã	eh ma**sa(n)**	apple
a mamã	eh ma**ma(n)**	Mummy
a mão	eh **mow(n)**	hand
as meias	ezh **may**esh	socks
a menina	eh me**nee**na	girl
o menino	oo me**nee**noo	boy
a mesa	eh **me**za	table
o nariz	oo na**reesh**	nose
os números	oozh **noo**meroosh	numbers
os olhos	ooz **ol**yoosh	eyes
as orelhas	ez o**reh**lyash	ears
a ovelha	eh o**veh**lya	sheep
o ovo	oo **o**voo	egg
os ovos	ooz **o**voosh	eggs
as pantufas	esh pan**too**fash	slippers
o pão	oo **pow(n)**	bread
o papá	oo pa**pa**	Daddy
o parque	oo **park**	park
o pássaro	oo **pas**saroo	bird
o patinho	oo pa**teen**yoo	duck
o peixe	oo **paysh**	fish
o pente	oo **pent**	comb
a perna	eh **pair**na	leg
os pés	oosh **pehsh**	feet
a piscina	eh pish**see**na	swimming pool
o porco	oo **por**coo	pig
a porta	eh **por**ta	door
o prato	oo **pra**too	plate
preto	**pre**too	black
o pulôver	oo pu**loh**ver	jumper
o quarto	oo **kwar**too	bedroom
quatro	**kwa**troo	four
o rabinho	oo ra**been**yoo	bottom
os rebuçados	oozh reboo**sah**doosh	sweets
o relógio	oo re**lo**zhioo	clock
a roupa	eh **roh**pa	clothes
a rua	eh **roo**-a	street
o sabonete	oo sabo**nett**	soap
a sala de estar	eh **sah**la de esh**tar**	living room
a sanita	eh sa**nee**ta	toilet
os sapatos	oosh sa**pah**toosh	shoes
a toalha	eh to-**ah**lya	towel
três	**traysh**	three
a T-shirt	eh **tee**-shirt	t-shirt
um (m) / uma (f)	**oom** / **oo**ma	one
o urso de peluche	oo **or**soo de pe**loosh**	teddy
a vaca	eh **va**ca	cow
verde	**verd**	green
vermelho	ver**meh**lyoo	red
o vestiário	oo vesh**tiah**rioo	changing room
o vestido	oo vesh**tee**doo	dress
a visita	eh vi**zee**ta	visit

First published in 2008 by Usborne Publishing Ltd, Usborne House, 83-85 Saffron Hill, London EC1N 8RT, England. www.usborne.com Copyright © 2008 Usborne Publishing Ltd. The name Usborne and the devices 🦋🎈 are Trade Marks of Usborne Publishing Ltd. All rights reserved. No part of this publication may be reproduced, stored in a retrieval system, or transmitted in any form or by any means, electronic, mechanical, photocopying, recording or otherwise without the prior permission of the publisher. Printed in China.